Terry,
Our very best wishes
for your birthday
Ellen & Graham Runciman
1975

D1252251

POEMS OF
HENRY LAWSON

POEMS OF
HENRY LAWSON

Selected by Walter Stone   Illustrated by Pro Hart

Ure Smith · Sydney

First published in Australia 1973
by Ure Smith Pty Limited
176 South Creek Road, Dee Why West 2099, Sydney
Paintings copyright © Pro Hart, 1973
Introduction copyright © Walter Stone, 1973
National Library of Australia Card
Number and ISBN 0 7254 0136 2
Designed in Australia
Printed in Singapore by
Kyodo-Shing Loong Printing Industries Pte Ltd

Fifth edition, 1974

Jacket painting: The Shearing-Shed
Oil on hardboard 14in x 23in 1973

The Poems

Introduction

In any part of Australia, almost in any company, the mere mention of Henry Lawson's name will bring an immediate response. Whether it gives rise to an anecdote or a recitation of a few lines of his verse or leads to a discussion of his place in Australian literature it will not pass unnoticed. Alone among our writers he takes his place not only as a writer but as part of the wide Australian tradition.

Few writers in their own time have been so popularly acclaimed and it may be argued that the unqualified adulation led indirectly to his later personal problems. In the literary world, as in all other walks of life, success fans the embers of jealousy and there were not wanting those who saw in his work the faults they failed to find in their own. If, as he did sometimes, smart under their attacks he fought back in caustic verse or prose, time proving him right. His work continues to excite, in different ways, each generation of readers.

The broad outlines of Henry Lawson's biography are now reasonably well documented but much minor detail, vital if we are to have a clear picture of his life and times, remains a blend of fact and fiction which only the intensive research of scholars such as Professor Colin Roderick will sort out. Contradictions and absurdities abound in much that has already been published and will continue to turn up as hitherto unpublished sources such as the private correspondence of his friends and others become available.

So realistically did Lawson identify himself with the times, and the people and the places of which he wrote that it is all too easy to assume that he was indulging in covert autobiography. Much, for instance, may be read into the poem 'The Wander-Light' or the two parts of his 'Fragment of Autobiography' unless the reader is careful to remember that the naturally creative writer has a license to indulge his fancy.

If it pleased him to claim a gypsy ancestry or to infer that he had been harshly treated by some of his friends, he did so careless of the fact that some day the truth would be known. If the facts of his love affair with Hannah Thornburn have been coloured by his recollection or the imagination of his contemporaries it has to be said that the unhappy, wayward genius that was Henry Lawson is not to be tried on these counts but rather on his achievements as a writer of prose and of verse that gave direction and distinction to an indigenous and national Australian literature.

Henry Lawson was born in a tent on the Weddin Mountains alluvial goldfields near the small town of Grenfell, New South Wales, on 17 June 1867. He was the first child of the marriage of Niels Hertzberg Larsen (later anglicised to Lawson) and Louisa Albury, who had married in July of the previous year.

His father was born into a prominent family at Flademoen, Tromoy, Norway in

1832, and was a man of some education and taste who had been trained in maritime navigation. He left his homeland in 1853 vowing never to return, reputedly because of a blighted romance, and almost three years later turned up at Melbourne, where in company with a shipmate, John Henry William Slee, he deserted his ship to try his luck in the goldrushes. Just how far fortune favoured him in the next twelve years we do not know. About the year 1866 still suffering from gold fever, he arrived at the goldfields at New Pipeclay (now called Eurunderee) where Louisa, a daughter of Henry Albury, a bush worker turned shanty-keeper, was living.

One of a family of six daughters and a son, she had been born in 1848 at Mudgee, had received an education, reasonable for the times, at the local public school where her ability had not passed unnoticed by a teacher who encouraged her love of books. Little is known of the courtship of Louisa by Niels but marriage was a bitter experience for each of them.

The restless Niels, unable to resist the lure of gold, took Louisa to the Grenfell diggings and when, a few months later, his son was born he was registered as Henry Lawson. His father was shown as Peter Lawson, the name by which he was generally known in Australia. There is no record of Henry having been baptised and his occasional use of the second names Hertzberg or Archibald is based on a very dubious legend.

The Lawsons soon afterwards returned to Eurunderee where Peter took up a selection which turned out be very poor country. There he built a cottage of which only the brick chimney still stands, now cared for as a literary shrine.

Henry Lawson was to spend the impressionable years of his childhood here, broken only by a period at Gulgong in 'The Roaring Days' and an occasional holiday with his mother's people in Sydney and Wallerawang. Despite his claim that his home-life was unhappy because of the incompatibility of his parents, his childhood would have differed little from that of many other children in the bush — and the city, too.

If there were 'Ragged Schools' for the children in the poverty stricken areas of Sydney there were no schools in many settled parts of the country and the young Henry Lawson was already nine when a Provisional School, 'The Old Bark School', was opened at Eurunderee in October 1876. He, and one of his younger brothers, were among the first pupils. Peter and Louisa Lawson had played a prominent part in the agitation which resulted in the establishment of the school. The mother had, earlier, inspired in her children an interest in literature by reading to them every night. Lawson recalled that he could barely wait for nightfall to hear the continuation of some of the stories.

About this time Lawson's chronic and incurable deafness became apparent and despite the blame he laid on teachers for his failure as a scholar his affliction must have been a contributing factor.

Later, because of a difference of opinion with John Tierney, the local teacher, Louisa sent Henry to a Roman Catholic School at Mudgee. There he came under the influence of Charles Kevan, a district inspector of schools, who encouraged him in his reading and talked to him of poetry. Dickens, Defoe, Marcus Clarke, Boldrewood, Bret Harte and Poe interested him.

Not yet turned fourteen, Lawson's school days and childhood ended. Peter, having abandoned farming, had for some time been engaged in various building contracts in the district and needed his son's help. It meant that Henry was to spend much of his time away from home learning to become a housepainter, acquiring some skill as a carpenter, and broadening his knowledge of bush life.

In 1883 Louisa and Peter leased the property at Eurunderee and Louisa, her marriage at an end, went to Sydney. In no time she sent for Henry, still working with his father, to join her, hoping no doubt to save him from the aimless life of the average bushworker. Finally she and her family settled at 138 Phillip Street which was to become a meeting place for many of the radicals and reformers of the turbulent 1880s, some of whom were later to become public figures, as Louisa herself did.

In the meantime she had Henry apprenticed to coach-painting at the carriage works of Hudson Brothers, at Clyde, a suburb some distance from the city across which the boy had to walk in the early hours of the morning to catch his train. Thus he came face to face with slum life and the social injustices of the day. He attended night classes in the city after his long working day but failed to matriculate for Sydney University. About the same time he abandoned his apprenticeship, and became a painter's improver.

The influence of the groups among whom his mother and he moved soon showed in his youthful attempts to write militant verse and prose and in 1887 he wrote his first prose article for the *Republican*, a radical weekly in which Louisa had an interest and which she hoped her son would one day edit.

In June 1887 four lines of a poem, initialled H. L., appeared in the 'Answers to Correspondents' column in the *Bulletin* with the advice 'try again'. In the following October, whilst he was in Melbourne undergoing further futile treatment for his deafness, the same paper published his 'Song of the Republic'. By the end of the year two more poems had appeared over Lawson's name with a laudatory note referring to him as a youth of seventeen. He was in fact twenty but it was obvious that his work had caught the eye of J. F. Archibald, editor of the weekly *Bulletin* which, founded in 1880, was already shaping public opinion on a catchcry or slogan of 'Australia for the Australians'.

It encouraged, fostered, published and paid for poetry and prose with a regularity which attracted to its pages a group of writers who were ultimately to be known as 'the *Bulletin* school' and whose literary achievements are now regarded as the beginnings of an indigenous Australian literature.

The purely literary pages of the *Bulletin*, as distinct from the political and other sections, were not many but the quixotic and skilful Archibald kept a close watch over everything that appeared and continually advised and even schooled his contributors in the terse style which he demanded. Lawson was quick to learn and the time was not far ahead when he would be hailed as the most brilliant of the *Bulletin* authors.

Barely twenty-one when 'Faces in the Street' was published, almost overnight he was famous. In a single poem he had exposed socal injustice in stanzas far more inspiring than any leader writer in the daily press could have done. About this time, too, he was contributing articles to the *Republican* of which he was now the nominal editor and which he helped to print. Like most journals of its kind it had a short life, failing in 1888 shortly after his mother began her monthly paper,

The Dawn, under the pseudonym of 'Dora Falconer'. By now an ardent suffragette and fighter for women's rights, a role she was to play almost until her death in 1922, her paper was printed, published and managed almost entirely by women, except for one male who had had some printing experience. *The Dawn* existed for longer than seventeen years, closing down in 1905.

Established as a poet, Lawson was slow to turn to fiction and his first story, 'His Father's Mate' was not published until 22 December 1888. A few days later his father, who had proudly shown his son's story in the *Bulletin* to his friends, died at Mount Victoria. One of Lawson's props had given way for it is evident from the visits he made to his father, whose building contracts were now centred in the Blue Mountains, that there was a strong bond between the two men — one that Louisa had deliberately tried to break when she took Henry to live with her in Sydney. He was to admit that there were faults on both sides in the break-up of his parents' marriage but his emotionally charged story 'A Child in the Dark and a Foreign Father' would not have pleased his mother.

Measured in terms of income, the life of the freelance writer in the 1890s who sought to live by writing alone, was even more precarious than it is today. Lawson, despite his increasing popularity, was still eking out a penurious livelihood by working at his trade whenever work was available.

Bent on a journalistic career, he travelled to Western Australia where he found conditions no better than they were at Sydney. He did contribute a series of articles to the newly founded *Albany Observer*. A few months later, in 1891, he joined the short-lived Brisbane *Boomerang*, edited by Gresley Lukin, as a columnist, and was a staff writer for six months at a wage of £2 per week.

Insecure, dejected, and frustrated, already addicted to alcohol, Lawson never ceased to believe in his own ability as a writer and by 1892, the year in which Archibald sent him to the town of Bourke 500 miles from Sydney to report on the great drought of 1892-93, he was seriously mastering the short story. Bourke provided him with an insight into the unionism of the nomadic shearers and bush workers and their creed of mateship which he was to make an article of faith for Australia.

Still desperate, still drinking, but still a fervent radical, an attitude which undoubtedly limited his opportunities for employment, if nothing else did, in 1894 he helped his mother produce his first book, '*Short Stories in Prose and Verse*', at the office of the *Dawn*. It was favourably received despite an introduction deploring local and overseas attitudes to Australian writing, but at a retail price of 1/- it brought no financial return.

Well known and well liked in literary circles, friendly with Mary Gilmore, Victor Daley, E. J. Brady, Roderic Quinn and Le Gay Brereton, read, quoted and discussed wherever the *Bulletin*, the *Worker*, or John Norton's Sydney *Truth* were circulating, with a book of poems, '*In the Days When the World was Wide*' in print and '*While the Billy Boils*', a book of short stories, in the press, both from the already prestigious publishers, Angus & Robertson, Lawson was at the height of his powers. Both books consolidated his place in the affections of the Australian public.

In the midst of this personal excitement Lawson married Bertha Bredt, who had met him the year previously whilst on a visit to her mother, now married to William McNamara, a leading radical bookseller in Sydney, and like Lawson's mother, destined to carve out a career for herself and later to be known as The Mother of the Labor Party. Another of her daughters, Hilda, had married in 1895 John Thomas Lang, a future Premier of New South Wales.

The marriage of Henry and Bertha proved as unhappy as their mutual friends had warned it would. To get Henry away from temptation she had gone with him on desperate trips to Western Australia and New Zealand, where his son, James, was born in March 1898. Bland Holt, a generous actor-manager, had commissioned and paid Henry for a drama which proved unplayable, but the money thus earned provided them with the means to return to Sydney in April. Between drinking bouts Lawson continued to write but by the end of the year he was for a time in a clinic for inebriates — nor was it to be the only time.

Lawson was still in his early thirties when he sailed for London, the Mecca of all successful colonial authors, in April 1900, accompanied by his wife and two children, his daughter Bertha a month old. Armed with the inevitable letters of introduction to editors and agents, his expenses paid by friends and supporters, he would begin a new life.

For a time his high hopes, and those of his friends seemed justified. J. B. Pinker, London's leading literary agent, was managing his affairs, he had received encouragement from English critics and his stories were being published in leading periodicals. But loneliness and the climate told in the end and he began drinking heavily again. Bertha's health gave way under the strain and by the end of 1902 they were back in Sydney from what Lawson wrote later was 'the run to England that almost ruined me'. It did.

The bitter years were about to begin. His wife in 1903 obtained a judicial separation and failure to comply with a maintenance order resulted in Henry spending various terms, over a period of years, in Long Bay gaol.

His literary powers declined with a general breakdown in health and only occasionally did flashes of his former genius appear to delight his readers.

He came to rely as much on the bounty of his friends as he did on the small literary pension paid by the Federal Government on his behalf to his 'little landlady, Mrs Byers', at whose small cottage in Abbotsford he died on 2 September 1922.

Given a State funeral and buried in Waverley Cemetery, he was remembered on all sides as 'The People's Poet'. He would have liked that.

WALTER STONE

11

The Teams

A CLOUD of dust on the long, white road,
  And the teams go creeping on
Inch by inch with the weary load;
And by the power of the green-hide goad
  The distant goal is won.

With eyes half-shut to the blinding dust,
  And necks to the yokes bent low,
The beasts are pulling as bullocks must;
And the shining tires might almost rust
  While the spokes are turning slow.

With face half-hid by a broad-brimmed hat,
  That shades from the heat's white waves,
And shouldered whip, with its green-hide plait,
The driver plods with a gait like that
  Of his weary, patient slaves.

He wipes his brow, for the day is hot,
  And spits to the left with spite;
He shouts at Bally, and flicks at Scot,
And raises dust from the back of Spot,
  And spits to the dusty right.

He'll sometimes pause as a thing of form
  In front of a settler's door,
And ask for a drink, and remark "It's warm".
Or say "There's signs of a thunderstorm";
  But he seldom utters more.

The rains are heavy on roads like these
  And, fronting his lonely home,
For days together the settler sees
The waggons bogged to the axletrees,
  Or ploughing the sodden loam.

And then, when the roads are at their worst,
  The bushman's children hear
The cruel blows of the whips reversed
While bullocks pull as their hearts would burst,
  And bellow with pain and fear.

And thus—with glimpses of home and rest—
  Are the long, long journeys done;
And thus—'tis a thankless life at the best!—
Is Distance fought in the mighty West,
  And the lonely battle won.

THE TEAMS
Oil on hardboard 14 in. × 18 in. 1973

The Shearer's Dream

OH, I dreamt I shore in a shearin'-shed, and it was a dream of joy,
For every one of the rouseabouts was a girl dressed up as a boy—
Dressed up like a page in a pantomime, and the prettiest ever seen—
They had flaxen hair, they had coal-black hair—and every shade
between.

There was short, plump girls, there was tall, slim girls, and the
handsomest ever seen—
They was four-foot-five, they was six-foot high, and every height
between.

The shed was cooled by electric fans that was over every shoot;
The pens was of polished ma-ho-gany, and everything else to suit;
The huts had springs to the mattresses, and the tucker was simply
grand,
And every night by the billerbong we danced to a German band.

Our pay was the wool on the jumbucks' backs, so we shore till all
was blue—
The sheep was washed afore they was shore (and the rams was
scented too);
And we all of us wept when the shed cut out, in spite of the long,
hot days,
For every hour them girls waltzed in with whisky and beer on
tr-a-a-ays!

There was three of them girls to every chap, and as jealous as they
could be—
There was three of them girls to every chap, and six of 'em picked
on me;
We was draftin' them out for the homeward track and sharin' 'em
round like steam,
When I woke with me head in the blazin' sun to find 'twas a
shearer's dream.

THE SHEARER'S DREAM
Oil on hardboard 14 in. × 18 in. 1973

Jack Dunn
of Nevertire

It chanced upon the very day we'd got the shearing done,
A buggy brought a stranger to the West-o'-Sunday Run;
He had a round and jolly face, and sleek he was and stout—
He drove right up between the huts and called the super out.
We chaps were smoking after tea, and heard the swell inquire
For one as travelled by the name of "Dunn of Nevertire".
    Jack Dunn of Nevertire,
    Old Dunn of Nevertire;
There wasn't one of us but knew Jack Dunn of Nevertire.

"Jack Dunn of Nevertire," he said; "I was a mate of his;
And now it's twenty years since I set eyes upon his phiz.
There is no whiter man than Jack—no straighter south the line,
There is no hand in all the land I'd sooner grip in mine;
To help a mate in trouble Jack would go through flood and fire.
Great Scott! and don't you know the name of Dunn of Nevertire?
    Big Dunn of Nevertire,
    Long Jack from Nevertire;
He stuck to me through thick and thin, Jack Dunn of Nevertire.

"I did a wild and foolish thing while Jack and I were mates,
And I disgraced my guv'nor's name, an' wished to try the States.
My lamps were turned to Yankee-land, for I'd some people there.
And I was 'right' when someone sent the money for my fare;
I thought 'twas Dad, until I took the trouble to inquire
And found the man who sent the stuff was Dunn of Nevertire,
    Jack Dunn of Nevertire,
    Soft Dunn of Nevertire;
He'd won some money on a race—Jack Dunn of Nevertire.

"Now I've returned, by Liverpool, a swell of Yankee brand;
I reckon, guess, and kalkilate to wake my native land;
There is no better land, I swear, in all the wide world round—
I smelt the bush a month before we touched King George's Sound
And now I've come to settle down, the top of my desire
Is just to meet a mate o' mine called 'Dunn of Nevertire'.
    Was raised at Nevertire—
    The town of Nevertire;
He humped his bluey by the name of 'Dunn of Nevertire'.

"I've heard he's poor, and if he is, a proud old fool is he;
But, spite of that, I'll find a way to fix the old gumtree.
I've bought a station in the North—the best that could be had;
I want a man to pick the stock—I want a super bad;
I want no bully-brute to boss—no crawling, sneaking liar—
My station super's name shall be 'Jack Dunn of Nevertire!"
    Straight Dunn of Nevertire,
    Proud Jack from Nevertire;
I guess he's known up Queensland way—Jack Dunn of Nevertire."

JACK DUNN OF NEVERTIRE
Oil on hardboard 18 in. × 14 in. 1973

The super said, while to his face a strange expression came:
"I *think* I've seen the man you want, I *think* I know the name;
Had he a jolly kind of face, a free and careless way,
Grey eyes that always seemed to smile, and hair just turning grey—
Clean-shaved, except a light moustache, long-limbed, an' tough as
  wire?"
"THAT'S HIM! THAT'S DUNN!" the stranger roared, "Jack Dunn of
  Nevertire!"
    John Dunn of Nevertire,
    Jack D. from Nevertire,
They said I'd find him here, the cuss!—Jack Dunn of Nevertire.

"I'd know his walk," the stranger cried, "though sobered, I'll allow."
"I doubt it much," the boss replied, "he don't walk that way now."
"Perhaps he don't!" the stranger said, "if years were hard on Jack;
But, if he were a mile away, I swear I'd know his back."
"I doubt it much," the super said, and sadly puffed his briar,
"I guess he wears a pair of wings—Jack Dunn of Nevertire;
    Jack Dunn of Nevertire,
    Brave Dunn of Nevertire,
He caught a fever nursing me, Jack Dunn of Nevertire."

We took the stranger round to where a gum-tree stood alone,
And in the grass beside the trunk he saw a granite stone;
The names of Dunn and Nevertire were plainly written there—
"I'm all broke up," the stranger said, in sorrow and despair,
"I guess he has a wider run, the man that I require;
He's got a river-frontage now, Jack Dunn of Nevertire;
    Straight Dunn of Nevertire,
    White Jack from Nevertire,
I guess Saint Peter knew the name of 'Dunn of Nevertire'."

Eureka (A Fragment)

Roll up, Eureka's heroes, on that Grand Old Rush afar,
For Lalor's gone to join you in the big camp where you are;
Roll up and give him welcome such as only diggers can,
For well he battled for the rights of miner and of Man.
In that bright, golden country that lies beyond our sight,
The record of his honest life shall be his Miner's Right;
But many a bearded mouth shall twitch, and many a tear be shed,
And many a grey old digger sigh to hear that Lalor's dead.
Yet wipe your eyes, old fossikers, o'er worked-out fields that roam,
You need not weep at parting from a digger going home.

Now from the strange wild seasons past, the days of golden strife,
Now from the Roaring Fifties comes a scene from Lalor's life:
All gleaming white amid the shafts o'er gully, hill, and flat
Again I see the tents that form the camp at Ballarat.
I hear the shovels and the picks, and all the air is rife
With the rattle of the cradles and the sounds of digger-life;
The clatter of the windlass-boles, as spinning round they go,
And then the signal to his mate, the digger's cry, "Below!"
From many a busy pointing-forge the sound of labour swells,
The tinkling at the anvils is as clear as silver bells.
I hear the broken English from the mouth of many a one
From every state and nation that is known beneath the sun;
The homely tongue of Scotland and the brogue of Ireland blend
With the dialects of England, right from Berwick to Land's End;
And to the busy concourse here the States have sent a part,
The land of gulches that has been immortalized by Harte;
The land where long from mining-camps the blue smoke upward
    curled;
The land that gave the "Partner" true and "Mliss" unto the world;
The men from all the nations in the New World and the Old,
All side by side, like brethren here, are delving after gold.
But suddenly the warning cries are heard on every side
As, closing in around the field, a ring of troopers ride.
Unlicensed diggers are the game—their class and want are sins,
And so, with all its shameful scenes, the digger-hunt begins.
The men are seized who are too poor the heavy tax to pay,
Chained man to man as convicts were, and dragged in gangs away.
Though in the eye of many a man the menace scarce was hid,
The diggers' blood was slow to boil, but scalded when it did.

But now another match is lit that soon must fire the charge,
A digger murdered in the camp; his murderer at large!
"Roll up! Roll up!" the poignant cry awakes the evening air,
And angry faces surge like waves around the speakers there.
"What are our sins that we should be an outlawed class?" they say,
"Shall we stand by while mates are seized and dragged like lags away?
Shall insult be on insult heaped? Shall we let these things go?"

And with a roar of voices comes the diggers' answer—"No!"
The day has vanished from the scene, but not the air of night
Can cool the blood that, ebbing back, leaves brows in anger white.
Lo, from the roof of Bentley's inn the flames are leaping high;
They write "Revenge!" in letters red across the smoke-dimmed sky.
"To arms! To arms!" the cry is out; "To arms and play your part;
For every pike upon a pole will find a tyrant's heart!"
Now Lalor comes to take the lead, the spirit does not lag,
And down the rough, wild diggers kneel beneath the Diggers' Flag;
Then, rising to their feet, they swear, while rugged hearts beat high,
To stand beside their leader and to conquer or to die!
Around Eureka's stockade now the shades of night close fast,
Three hundred sleep beside their arms, and thirty sleep their last.

About the streets of Melbourne town the sound of bells is borne
That call the citizens to prayer that fateful Sabbath morn;
But there, upon Eureka's hill, a hundred miles away,
The diggers' forms lie white and still above the blood-stained clay.
The bells that toll the diggers' death might also ring a knell
For those few gallant soldiers, dead, who did their duty well.
The sight of murdered heroes is to hero-hearts a goad,
A thousand men are up in arms upon the Creswick road,
And wildest rumours in the air are flying up and down,
'Tis said the men of Ballarat will march on Melbourne town.
But not in vain those diggers died. Their comrades may rejoice,
For o'er the voice of tyranny is heard the people's voice;
It says: "Reform your rotten law, the diggers' wrongs make right,
Or else with them, our brothers now, we'll gather to the fight."

'Twas of such stuff the men were made who saw our nation born,
And such as Lalor were the men who led the vanguard on;
And like such men may we be found, with leaders such as they,
In the roll-up of Australians on our darkest, grandest day!

EUREKA
Oil on hardboard 18 in. × 14 in. 1973

The Wander-Light

Oh, my ways are strange ways and new ways and old ways,
And deep ways and steep ways and high ways and low;
I'm at home and at ease on a track that I know not
And restless and lost on a road that I know.

Then they heard the tent-poles clatter,
    And the fly in twain was torn—
'Twas the soiled rag of a tatter
    Of the tent where I was born.
Does it matter? Which is stranger—
    Brick or stone or calico?—
There was One born in a manger
    Nineteen hundred years ago.

For my beds were camp beds and tramp beds and damp beds,
And my beds were dry beds on drought-stricken ground,
Hard beds and soft beds, and wide beds and narrow—
For my beds were strange beds the wide world round.

And the old hag seemed to ponder
    With her grey head nodding slow—
"He will dream, and he will wander
    Where but few would think to go.
He will flee the haunts of tailors,
    He will cross the ocean wide,
For his fathers they were sailors—
    All on his good father's side."

I rest not, 'tis best not, the world is a wide one—
And, caged for a moment, I pace to and fro;
I see things and dree things and plan while I'm sleeping,
I wander for ever and dream as I go.

And the old hag she was troubled
    As she bent above the bed;
"He will dream things and he'll see things
    To come true when he is dead.
He will see things all too plainly,
    And his fellows will deride,
For his mothers they were gipsies—
    All on his good mother's side."

And my dreams are strange dreams, are day dreams, are grey dreams,
And my dreams are wild dreams, and old dreams and new;
They haunt me and daunt me with fears of the morrow—
My brothers they doubt me—but my dreams come true.

THE WANDER-LIGHT
Oil on hardboard 14 in. × 10 in. 1973

The Shearing-Shed

"THE ladies are coming," the super says
    To the shearers sweltering there,
And "the ladies" means in the shearing-shed:
    "Don't cut 'em too bad. Don't swear."
The ghost of a pause in the shed's rough heart,
    And lower is bowed each head;
Then nothing is heard save a whispered word
    And the roar of the shearing-shed.

The tall, shy rouser has lost his wits;
    His limbs are all astray;
He leaves a fleece on the shearing-board
    And his broom in the shearer's way.
There's a curse in store for that jackeroo
    As down by the wall he slants—
But the ringer bends with his legs askew
    And wishes he'd "patched them pants".

They are girls from the city. Our hearts rebel
    As we squint at their dainty feet,
While they gush and say in a girly way
    That "the dear little lambs" are "sweet".
And Bill the Ringer, who'd scorn the use
    Of a childish word like damn,
Would give a pound that his tongue were loose
    As he tackles a lively lamb.

Swift thought of home in the coastal towns—
    Or rivers and waving grass—
And a weight on our hearts that we cannot define
    That comes as the ladies pass;
But the rouser ventures a nervous dig
    With his thumb in the next man's back;
And Bogan says to his pen-mate: "Twig
    The style of that last un, Jack."

Jack Moonlight gives her a careless glance—
    Then catches his breath with pain;
His strong hand shakes, and the sunbeams dance
    As he bends to his work again.
But he's well disguised in a bristling beard,
    Bronzed skin, and his shearer's dress;
And whatever he knew or hoped or feared
    Was hard for his mates to guess.

THE SHEARING-SHED
Oil on hardboard 14 in. × 18 in. 1973

Jack Moonlight, wiping his broad, white brow,
   Explains, with a doleful smile,
"A stitch in the side," and "I'm all right now"—
   But he leans on the beam awhile,
And gazes out in the blazing noon
   On the clearing, brown and bare . . . .
She had come and gone—like a breath of June
   In December's heat and glare.

Trooper Campbell

ONE day old Trooper Campbell
   Rode out to Blackman's Run;
His cap-peak and his sabre
   Were glancing in the sun.
'Twas New Year's Eve, and slowly
   Across the ridges low
The sad Old Year was drifting
   To where the old years go.

The trooper's mind was reading
   The love-page of his life—
His love for Mary Wylie
   Ere she was Blackman's wife;
He sorrowed for the sorrows
   Of the heart a rival won,
For he knew that there was trouble
   Out there on Blackman's Run.

The sapling shades had lengthened,
   The summer day was late,
When Blackman met the trooper
   Beyond the homestead gate;
And, if the hand of trouble
   Can leave a lasting trace,
The lines of care had come to stay
   On poor old Blackman's face.

"Not good day, Trooper Campbell,
   It's a bad, bad day for me—
You are of all the men on earth
   The one I wished to see.
The great black clouds of trouble
   Above our homestead hang;
That wild and reckless boy of mine
   Has joined M'Durmer's gang.

"Oh! save him, save him, Campbell,
   I beg in friendship's name!
For if they take and hang him,
   The wife would die of shame.
Could Mary and her sisters
   Hold up their heads again,
And face a woman's malice,
   Or claim the love of men?

"And if he does a murder
   We all were better dead.
Don't take him living, Trooper,
   If a price be on his head;
But shoot him! shoot him, Campbell,

When you meet him face to face,
  And save him from the gallows—
    And us from that disgrace."

"Now, Tom," cried Trooper Campbell,
  "You know your words are wild.
Wild though he is and reckless,
  Yet still he is your child;
Bear up and face your trouble,
  Yes, meet it like a man,
And tell the wife and daughters
  I'll save him if I can."

The sad Australian sunset
  Had faded from the west;
But night brought darker shadows
  To hearts that could not rest;
And Blackman's wife sat rocking
  And moaning in her chair.
"Oh, the disgrace, disgrace," she moaned;
  "It's more than I can bear.

"In hardship and in trouble
  I struggled year by year
To make my children better
  Than other children here.
And if my son's a felon
  How can I show my face?
I cannot bear disgrace; my God,
  I cannot bear disgrace!

"Ah, God in Heaven pardon!
  I'm selfish in my woe—
My boy is better-hearted
  Than many that I know.
I'll face whatever happens,
  And, till his mother's dead,
My foolish child shall find a place
  To lay his outlawed head."

Sore-hearted, Trooper Campbell
  Rode out from Blackman's Run,
Nor noticed aught about him
  Till thirteen miles were done;
When, close beside a cutting,
  He heard the click of locks,
And saw the rifle-muzzles
  Trained on him from the rocks.

TROOPER CAMPBELL
Oil on hardboard 14 in. × 18 in. 1973

But suddenly a youth rode out,
    And, close by Campbell's side:
"Don't fire! don't fire, in Heaven's name!
    It's Campbell, boys!" he cried.
Then one by one in silence
    The levelled rifles fell,
For who'd shoot Trooper Campbell
    Of those who knew him well?

On, bravely sat old Campbell,
    No sign of fear showed he.
He slowly drew his carbine;
    It rested by his knee.
The outlaws' guns were lifted,
    But none the silence broke,
Till steadfastly and firmly
    Old Trooper Campbell spoke,

"The boy that you would ruin
    Goes home with me, my men;
Or some of us shall never
    Ride through the Gap again.
You all know Trooper Campbell,
    And have you ever heard
That bluff or lead could turn him
    Or make him break his word?

"That reckless lad is playing
    A heartless villain's part;
He knows that he is breaking
    His poor old mother's heart.
He's going straight to ruin;
    But 'tis not that alone,
He'll bring dishonour to a name
    That I'd be proud to own.

"I speak to you, M'Durmer—
    If your heart's not granite quite,
And if you'd seen the trouble
    At Blackman's home tonight,
You'd help me now, M'Durmer—
    I speak as man to man—
I swore to save the foolish lad—
    I'll save him if I can."

"Oh, take him!" said M'Durmer, ,
    He's got a horse to ride . . . ."
The youngster thought a moment,
    Then rode to Campbell's side . . . .
"Good-bye!" young Blackman shouted,

As up the range they sped.
"Luck for the New Year, Campbell,"
    Was all M'Durmer said.

Then fast along the ridges
    Two horsemen rode a race,
The moonlight lent a glory
    To Trooper Campbell's face.
And ere the new year's dawning
    They reached the homestead gate—
"I found him," said the Trooper,
    "And not, thank God, too late!"

The Sliprails and the Spur

THE colours of the setting sun
  Withdrew across the Western land—
He raised the sliprails, one by one,
  And shot them home with trembling hand;
Her brown hands clung—her face grew pale—
  Ah! quivering chin and eyes that brim!—
One quick, fierce kiss across the rail,
  And, "Good-bye, Mary!" "Good-bye, Jim!"

Oh, he rides hard to race the pain
  Who rides from love, who rides from home;
But he rides slowly home again,
  Whose heart has learnt to love and roam.

A hand upon the horse's mane,
  And one foot in the stirrup set,
And, stooping back to kiss again,
  With "Good-bye, Mary! don't you fret!
When I come back"—he laughed for her—
  "We do not know how soon 'twill be;
I'll whistle as I round the spur—
  You let the sliprails down for me."

She gasped for sudden loss of hope,
  As, with a backward wave to her,
He cantered down the grassy slope
  And swiftly round the darkening spur.
Black-pencilled panels standing high,
  And darkness fading into stars,
And, blurring fast against the sky,
  A faint white form beside the bars.

And often at the set of sun,
  In winter bleak and summer brown,
She'd steal across the little run,
  And shyly let the sliprails down,
And listen there when darkness shut
  The nearer spur in silence deep,
And when they called her from the hut
  Steal home and cry herself to sleep.

And he rides hard to dull the pain
  Who rides from one that loves him best . . .
And he rides slowly back again,
  Whose restless heart must rove for rest.

THE SLIPRAILS AND THE SPUR
Oil on hardboard 18 in. × 14 in. 1973

The Lights of Cobb and Co.

FIRE lighted; on the table a meal for sleepy men;
A lantern in the stable; a jingle now and then;
The mail-coach looming darkly by light of moon and star;
The growl of sleepy voices; a candle in the bar;
A stumble in the passage of folk with wits abroad;
A swear-word from a bedroom—the shout of "All aboard!"
"Tchk tchk! Git-up!" "Hold fast, there!" and down the range we go;
Five hundred miles of scattered camps will watch for Cobb and Co.

Old coaching towns already decaying for their sins;
Uncounted "Half-Way Houses", and scores of "Ten-Mile Inns";
The riders from the stations by lonely granite peaks;
The black-boy for the shepherds on sheep and cattle creeks;
The roaring camps of Gulgong, and many a "Digger's Rest";
The diggers on the Lachlan; the huts of Farthest West;
Some twenty thousand exiles who sailed for weal or woe—
The bravest hearts of twenty lands will wait for Cobb and Co.

The morning star has vanished, the frost and fog are gone,
In one of those grand mornings which but on mountains dawn;
A flask of friendly whisky—each other's hopes we share—
And throw our top-coats open to drink the mountain air.
The roads are rare to travel, and life seems all complete;
The grind of wheels on gravel, the trot of horses' feet,
The trot, trot, trot and canter, as down the spur we go—
The green sweeps to horizons blue that call for Cobb and Co.

We take a bright girl actress through western dusts and damps,
To bear the home-world message, and sing for sinful camps,
To stir our hearts and break them, wild hearts that hope and ache—
(Ah! when she thinks again of these her own must nearly break!)
Five miles this side the gold-field, a loud, triumphant shout:
Five hundred cheering diggers have snatched the horses out:
With "Auld Lang Syne" in chorus, through roaring camps they go
That cheer for her, and cheer for Home, and cheer for Cobb and Co.

Three lamps above the ridges and gorges dark and deep,
A flash on sandstone cuttings where sheer the sidlings sweep,
A flash on shrouded waggons, on water ghastly white;
Weird bush and scattered remnants of "rushes in the night";
Across the swollen river a flash beyond the ford:
Ride hard to warn the driver! He's drunk or mad, good Lord!
But on the bank to westward a broad and cheerful glow—
New camps extend across the plains new routes for Cobb and Co.

THE LIGHTS OF COBB AND CO.
Oil on hardboard 16 in. × 20 in. 1973

Swift scramble up the sidling where teams climb inch by inch;
Pause, bird-like, on the summit—then breakneck down the pinch;
By clear, ridge-country rivers, and gaps where tracks run high,
Where waits the lonely horseman, cut clear against the sky;
Past haunted half-way houses—where convicts made the bricks—
Scrub-yards and new bark shanties, we dash with five and six;
Through stringy-bark and blue-gum, and box and pine we go—
A hundred miles shall see tonight the lights of Cobb and Co.!

Song of Old Joe Swallow

When I was up the country in the rough and early days,
I used to work along of Jimmy Nowlett's bullick-drays;
Then the reelroad wasn't heered on, an' the bush was wild an' strange,
An' we useter draw the timber from the saw-pits in the range—
Load provisions for the stations, an' we'd travel far and slow
Through the plains an' 'cross the ranges in the days of long ago.

Then it's yoke up the bullicks and tramp beside 'em slow,
An' saddle up yer horses an' a-ridin' we well go,
To the bullick-drivin', cattle-drovin'
Nigger, digger, roarin', rovin'
Days o' long ago.

Once me an Jimmy Nowlett loaded timber for the town,
But we hadn't gone a dozen mile before the rain come down,
An' me an' Jimmy Nowlett an' the bullicks an' the dray
Was cut off on some risin' ground while floods around us lay;
An' we soon run short of tucker an' terbaccer, which was bad,
An' pertaters dipped in honey was the only tuck we had.

Then half our bullicks perished, when a drought was on the land,
In the burnin' heat that dazzles as it dances on the sand;
But in spite of barren ridges, an' in spite of mud, an' heat,
An' the dust that browned the bushes when it rose from bullicks' feet,
An' in spite of modern progress, and in spite of all their blow,
'Twas a better land to live in, in the days o' long ago.

When the frosty moon was shinin' o'er the ranges like a lamp,
An' a lot of bullick-drivers was a-campin' on the camp,
When the fire was blazin' cheery an' the pipes was drawin' well,
Then our songs we useter chorus an' our yarns we useter tell;
An' we'd talk of lands we come from, and of chaps we useter know,
For there always was behind us other days o' long ago.

Ah, them early days was ended when the reelroad crossed the plain,
But in dreams I often tramp beside the bullick-team again:
Still we pauses at the shanty just to have a drop o' cheer,
Still I feels a kind of pleasure when the campin'-ground is near;
Still I smells the old tarpaulin me an Jimmy useter throw
'Cross the timber-track for shelter in the days of long ago.

I have been a-drifting back'ards with the changes of the land,
An' if I spoke to bullicks now they wouldn't understand;
But when Mary wakes me sudden in the night I'll often say:
"Come here, Spot, an' stan' up, Bally, blank an' blank an' come-
      eer-way."
An' she says that, when I'm sleepin', oft my elerquince 'ill flow
In the bullick-drivin' language of the days o' long ago.

Well, the pub will soon be closin', so I'll give the thing a rest;
But if you should drop on Nowlett in the far an' distant west—
An' if Jimmy uses doubleyou instead of ar or vee,
An' if he drops his aitches, then you're sure to know it's he.
An' you won't forgit to arsk him if he still remembers Joe.
As knowed him up the country in the days o' long ago.

Then it's yoke up the bullicks and tramp beside
*   em slow,*
An' saddle up yer horses an' a-ridin' we will go,
To the bullick-drivin', cattle-drovin'
Nigger, digger, roarin', rovin'
Days o' long ago.

SONG OF OLD JOE SWALLOW
Oil on hardboard 14 in. × 18 in. 1973

39

Andy's Gone With Cattle

OUR Andy's gone with cattle now—
 Our hearts are out of order—
With drought he's gone to battle now
 Across the Queensland border.

He's left us in dejection now;
 Our thoughts with him are roving;
It's dull on this selection now,
 Since Andy went a-droving.

Who now shall wear the cheerful face
 In times when things are slackest?
And who shall whistle round the place
 When Fortune frowns her blackest?

Oh, who shall cheek the squatter now
 When he comes round us snarling?
His tongue is growing hotter now
 Since Andy crossed the Darling.

Oh, may the showers in torrents fall,
 And all the tanks run over;
And may the grass grow green and tall
 In pathways of the drover;

And may good angels send the rain
 On desert stretches sandy;
And when the summer comes again
 God grant 'twill bring us Andy.

ANDY'S GONE WITH CATTLE
Oil on hardboard 14 in. × 18 in. 1973

The Glass on the Bar

THREE bushmen one morning rode up to an inn,
And one of them call for the drinks with a grin;
They'd only returned from a trip to the North,
And, eager to greet them, the landlord came forth.
He absently poured out a glass of Three Star,
And set down that drink with the rest on the bar.

"There, that is for Harry," he said, "and it's queer,
'Tis the very same glass that he drank from last year;
His name's on the glass, you can read it like print,
He scratched it himself with an old bit of flint;
I remember his drink — it was always Three Star" —
And the landlord looked out through the door of the bar.

He looked at the horses, and counted but three:
"You were always together—where's Harry?" cried he.
Oh, sadly they looked at the glass as they said,
"You may put it away, for our old mate is dead;"
But one, gazing out o'er the ridges afar,
Said, "We owe him a shout—leave the glass on the bar."

They thought of the far-away grave on the plain,
They thought of the comrade who came not again,
They lifted their glasses, and sadly they said:
"We drink to the name of the mate who is dead."
And the sunlight streamed in, and a light like a star
Seemed to glow in the depth of the glass on the bar.

And still in that shanty a tumbler is seen,
It stands by the clock, always polished and clean;
And often the strangers will read as they pass
The name of a bushman engraved on the glass;
And though on the shelf but a dozen there are,
That glass never stands with the rest on the bar.

THE GLASS ON THE BAR
Oil on hardboard 14 in. × 18 in. 1973

The Cattle-Dog's Death

THE plains lay bare on the homeward route, .
And the march was heavy on man and brute;
For the Spirit of Drouth was on all the land,
And the white heat danced on the glowing sand.

The best of our cattle-dogs lagged at last;
His strength gave out ere the plains were passed;
And our hearts were sad as he crept and laid
His languid limbs in the nearest shade.

He saved our lives in the years gone by,
When no one dreamed of the danger nigh,
And treacherous blacks in the darkness crept
On the silent camp where the white men slept.

"Rover is dying," a stockman said,
As he knelt and lifted the shaggy head;
"'Tis a long day's march ere the run be near,
And he's going fast; shall we leave him here?"

But the super cried, "There's an answer there!"
As he raised a tuft of the dog's grey hair;
And, strangely vivid, each man descried
The old spear-mark on the shaggy hide.

We laid a bluey and coat across
A camp-pack strapped on the lightest horse,
Then raised the dog to his deathbed high,
And brought him far 'neath the burning sky.

At the kindly touch of the stockmen rude
His eyes grew human with gratitude;
And though we were parched, when his eyes grew dim
The last of our water was given to him.

The super's daughter we knew would chide
If we left the dog in the desert wide;
So we carried him home o'er the burning sand
For a parting stroke from her small white hand.

But long ere the station was seen ahead,
His pain was o'er, for Rover was dead;
And the folks all knew by our looks of gloom
'Twas a comrade's corpse that we carried home.

THE CATTLE-DOG'S DEATH
Oil on hardboard 14 in. × 18 in. 1973

Mary Called Him Mister

THEY'D parted just a year ago—she thought he'd ne'er come back;
She stammered, blushed, held out her hand, and called him "Mister
  Mack".
How could he know that all the while she longed to murmur "John"?-
He called her "Miss le Brook", and asked "How she was getting on".

They'd parted but a year before; they'd loved each other well,
But he'd been down to Sydney since, and come back *such* a swell.
They longed to meet in fond embrace, they hungered for a kiss —
But Mary called him *Mister*, and the idiot called her *Miss*.

He paused, and leaned against the door—a stupid chap was he—
And, when she asked if he'd come in and have a cup of tea,
He looked to left, he looked to right, and then he glanced behind . . .
And slowly doffed his cabbage-tree . . . and said he "didn't mind".

She made a shy apology because the meat was tough,
Then asked if he was quite, quite sure the tea was sweet enough;
He stirred his tea, and sipped it twice, and answered "plenty quite".
And cut himself a slice of beef, and said that it was "right".

She glanced at him, at times, and coughed an awkward little cough;
He stared at anything but her and said, "I must be off".
That evening he went riding north—a sad and lonely ride—
She locked herself inside her room, and sat her down and cried.

They'd parted but a year before, they loved each other well—
But she was *such* a country girl and he'd grown such a swell;
They longed to meet in fond embrace, they hungered for a kiss—
But Mary called him *Mister*, and the idiot called her *Miss*.

MARY CALLED HIM MISTER
Oil on hardboard 14 in. × 18 in. 1973

Song of the Old Bullock-Driver

FAR back in the days when the blacks used to ramble
   In long single file 'neath the evergreen tree,
The wool-teams in season came down from Coonamble,
   And journeyed for weeks on their way to the sea.
'Twas then that our hearts and our sinews were stronger,
   For those were the days when tough bushmen were bred.
We journeyed on roads that were rougher and longer
   Than roads which the feet of our grandchildren tread.

We never were lonely, for, camping together,
   We yarned and we smoked the long evenings away,
And little I cared for the signs of the weather
   When snug in my hammock slung under the dray.
We rose with the dawn, were it ever so chilly,
   When yokes and tarpaulins were covered with frost,
And toasted the bacon and boiled the black billy—
   Then high on the camp-fire the branches we tossed.

On flats where the air was suggestive of possums,
   And homesteads and fences were hinting of change,
We saw the faint glimmer of apple-tree blossoms,
   And far in the distance the blue of the range;
Out there in the rain there was small use in flogging
   The poor tortured bullocks that tugged at the load,
When down to the axles, the waggons were bogging
   And traffic was making a slough of the road.

Oh, hard on the beasts were those terrible pinches
   Where two teams of bullocks were yoked to a load,
And tugging and slipping, and moving by inches,
   Half-way to the summit they clung to the road.
And then, when the last of the pinches was bested,
   (You'll surely not say that a glass was a sin?)
The bullocks lay down 'neath the gum-trees and rested—
   The bullockies steered for the door of the inn.

Then slowly we crawled by the trees that kept tally
   Of miles that were passed on the long journey down.
We saw the wild beauty of Capertee Valley,
   As slowly we rounded the base of the Crown.
But, ah! the poor bullocks were cruelly goaded
   While climbing the hills from the flats and the vales;
'Twas here that the teams were so often unloaded
   That all knew the meaning of "counting your bales".

SONG OF THE OLD BULLOCK-DRIVER
Oil on hardboard 14 in. × 18 in. 1973

The best-paying load that I ever have carried
    Was the one to the run where my sweetheart was nurse.
We courted awhile, and agreed to get married,
    And couple our futures for better or worse.
And when my old feet were too weary to drag on
    The miles of rough metal they met by the way,
My eldest grew up and I gave him the waggon—
    He's plodding along by the bullocks today.

Ballad of the Drover

ACROSS the stony ridges,
　Across the rolling plain,
Young Harry Dale, the drover,
　Comes riding home again.
And well his stock-horse bears him,
　And light of heart is he,
And stoutly his old packhorse
　Is trotting by his knee.

Up Queensland way with cattle
　He's travelled regions vast,
And many months have vanished
　Since home-folks saw him last.
He hums a song of someone
　He hopes to marry soon;
And hobble-chains and camp-ware
　Keep jingling to the tune.

Beyond the hazy dado
　Against the lower skies
And yon blue line of ranges
　The station homestead lies.
And thitherward the drover
　Jogs through the lazy noon,
While hobble-chains and camp-ware
　Are jingling to a tune.

An hour has filled the heavens
　With storm-clouds inky black;
At times the lightning trickles
　Around the drover's track;
But Harry pushes onward,
　His horses' strength he tries,
In hope to reach the river
　Before the flood shall rise.

The thunder, pealing o'er him,
　Goes rumbling down the plain;
And sweet on thirsty pastures
　Beats fast the plashing rain;
Then every creek and gully
　Sends forth its tribute flood—
The river runs a banker,
　All stained with yellow mud.

Now Harry speaks to Rover,
　The best dog on the plains,

And to his hardy horses,
  And strokes their shaggy manes:
"We've breasted bigger rivers
  When floods were at their height,
Nor shall this gutter stop us
  From getting home tonight!"

The thunder growls a warning
  The blue, forked lightnings gleam;
The drover turns his horses
  To swim the fatal stream.
But, oh! the flood runs stronger
  Than e'er it ran before;
The saddle-horse is failing,
  And only half-way o'er!

When flashes next the lightning,
  The flood's grey breast is blank;
A cattle-dog and packhorse
  Are struggling up the bank.
But in the lonely homestead
  The girl shall wait in vain—
He'll never pass the stations
  In charge of stock again.

The faithful dog a moment
  Lies panting on the bank,
Then plunges through the current
  To where his master sank.
And round and round in circles
  He fights with failing strength,
Till, gripped by wilder waters,
  He fails and sinks at length.

Across the flooded lowlands
  And slopes of sodden loam
The packhorse struggles bravely
  To take dumb tidings home;
And mud-stained, wet, and weary,
  He goes by rock and tree,
With clanging chains and tinware
  All sounding eerily.

BALLAD OF THE DROVER
Oil on hardboard 14 in. × 18 in. 1973

Sticking to Bill

THERE'S a thing that sends a lump to my throat,
    And cuts my heart like a knife:
'Tis the woman who waits at the prison gate,
    When the woman is not his wife.
You may preach and pray till the dawn of day,
    Denounce or damn as you will,
But the soul of that woman will cleave for aye
    To the sin-stained soul of Bill.

She has no use for our sympathy
    And her face is hard as a stone—
A rag of a woman, at war with the world
    And fiercely fighting alone.
At the kindly touch of the janitor's hand
    The eyes of a wife would fill,
But Sal replies with a "Blast yer eyes!"—
    She is only stickin' to Bill.

In spite of herself there is help that comes—
    And it comes from a source well hid—
To buy the tucker and pay the rent
    Of a roost for herself and kid.
For the "talent" has sent round its thievish hat
    By one with a fist and a will,
For a quid or two just to see Sal through—
    For Sal is stickin' to Bill.

A furtive figure from Nowhere comes
    To Red Rock Lane by night,
And it softly raps at a dingy door
    While it scowls to left and right:
It jerks its arm in a half salute,
    By habit—against its will;
'Tis a fellow felon of Bill's, discharged,
    And it brings her a message from Bill.

There's a woman who comes to the gate alone
    (Bill's Gaol Delivery's near),
With a face a little less like a stone
    And a sign of a savage tear;
With a suit of clobber done up and darned—
    For William is leaving "The Hill",
And the tear is the first she ever has shed
    Since she's been stickin' to Bill.

STICKING TO BILL
Oil on hardboard 14 in. × 18 in. 1973

There's tucker at home, and a job to come
    And no one to wish him ill,
There's a bottle of beer, and a minded kid
    In a brand-new suit of drill.
There's an old-time mate who will steer him straight,
    And the sticks of furniture still—
He can take a spell for a month if he likes,
    And—she's done her best for Bill.

Faces in the Street

THEY lie, the men who tell us, for reasons of their own,
That want is here a stranger, and that misery's unknown;
For where the nearest suburb and the city proper meet
My window-sill is level with the faces in the street—
      Drifting past, drifting past,
      To the beat of weary feet—
While I sorrow for the owners of those faces in the street.

And cause I have to sorrow, in a land so young and fair,
To see upon those faces stamped the marks of Want and Care;
I look in vain for traces of the fresh and fair and sweet
In sallow, sunken faces that are drifting through the street—
      Drifting on, drifting on,
      To the scrape of restless feet;
I can sorrow for the owners of the faces in the street.

In hours before the dawning dims the starlight in the sky
The wan and weary faces first begin to trickle by,
Increasing as the moments hurry on with morning feet,
Till like a pallid river flow the faces in the street—
      Flowing in, flowing in,
      To the beat of hurried feet—
Ah! I sorrow for the owners of those faces in the street.

The human river dwindles when 'tis past the hour of eight,
Its waves go flowing faster in the fear of being late;
But slowly drag the moments, whilst beneath the dust and heat
The city grinds the owners of the faces in the street—
      Grinding body, grinding soul,
      Yielding scarce enough to eat—
Oh! I sorrow for the owners of the faces in the street.

And then the only faces till the sun is sinking down
Are those of outside toilers and the idlers of the town,
Save here and there a face that seems a stranger in the street
Tells of the city's unemployed upon their weary beat—
      Drifting round, drifting round,
      To the tread of listless feet—
Ah! my heart aches for the owner of that sad face in the street.

And when the hours on lagging feet have slowly dragged away,
And sickly yellow gaslights rise to mock the going day,
Then, flowing past my window, like a tide in its retreat,
Again I see the pallid stream of faces in the street—
      Ebbing out, ebbing out,
      To the drag of tired feet,
While my heart is aching dumbly for the faces in the street.

And now all blurred and smirched with vice the day's sad end is seen,
For where the short "large hours" against the longer "small hours" lea
With smiles that mock the wearer, and with words that half entreat,
Delilah pleads for custom at the corner of the street—
　　　Sinking down, sinking down,
　　　Battered wreck by tempests beat—
A dreadful, thankless trade is hers, that Woman of the Street.

But, ah! to dreader things than these our fair young city comes,
For in its heart are growing thick the filthy dens and slums,
Where human forms shall rot away in sties for swine unmeet
And ghostly faces shall be seen unfit for any street—
　　　Rotting out, rotting out,
　　　For the lack of air and meat—
In dens of vice and horror that are hidden from the street.

I wonder would the apathy of the wealthy men endure
Were all their windows level with the faces of the Poor?
Ah! Mammon's slaves, your knees shall knock, your hearts in terror bea
When God demands a reason for the sorrows of the street,
　　　The wrong things and the bad things
　　　And the sad things that we meet
In the filthy lane and alley, and the cruel, heartless street.

I left the dreadful corner where the steps are never still,
And sought another window overlooking gorge and hill;
But when the night came dreary with the driving rain and sleet,
They haunted me—the shadows of those faces in the street,
　　　Flitting by, flitting by,
　　　Flitting by with noiseless feet,
And with cheeks that scarce were paler than the real ones in the street.

Once I cried: "O God Almighty! if Thy might doth still endure,
Now show me in a vision for the wrongs of Earth a cure."
And, lo, with shops all shuttered I beheld a city's street,
And in the warning distance heard the tramp of many feet,
　　　Coming near, coming near,
　　　To a drum's dull distant beat—
'Twas Despair's conscripted army that was marching down the street!

Then, like a swollen river that has broken bank and wall,
The human flood came pouring with the red flags over all,
And kindled eyes all blazing bright with revolution's heat,
And flashing swords reflecting rigid faces in the street—
　　　Pouring on, pouring on,
　　　To a drum's loud threatening beat,
And the war-hymns and the cheering of the people in the street.

FACES IN THE STREET
Oil on hardboard 14 in. × 18 in. 1973

And so it must be while the world goes rolling round its course,
The warning pen shall write in vain, the warning voice grow hoarse,
For not until a city feels Red Revolution's feet
Shall its sad people miss awhile the terrors of the street—
 The dreadful, everlasting strife
 For scarcely clothes and meat
In that pent track of living death—the city's cruel street.

Reedy River

TEN miles down Reedy River
    A pool of water lies,
And all the year it mirrors
    The changes in the skies.
Within that pool's broad bosom
    Is room for all the stars;
Its bed of sand has drifted
    O'er countless rocky bars.

Around the lower edges
    There waves a bed of reeds,
Where water-rats are hidden
    And where the wild-duck breeds;
And grassy slopes rise gently
    To ridges long and low,
Where groves of wattle flourish
    And native bluebells grow.

Beneath the granite ridges
    The eye may just discern
Where Rocky Creek emerges
    From deep green banks of fern;
And standing tall between them,
    The drooping sheoaks cool
The hard, blue-tinted waters
    Before they reach the pool.

Ten miles down Reedy River
    One Sunday afternoon,
I rode with Mary Campbell
    To that broad, bright lagoon;
We left our horses grazing
    Till shadows climbed the peak,
And strolled beneath the sheoaks
    On the banks of Rocky Creek.

Then home along the river
    That night we rode a race,
And the moonlight lent a glory
    To Mary Campbell's face;
I pleaded for my future
    All through that moonlight ride,
Until our weary horses
    Drew closer side by side.

Ten miles from Ryan's Crossing
    And five below the peak,

I built a little homestead
　　On the banks of Rocky Creek;
I cleared the land and fenced it
　　And ploughed the rich red loam;
And my first crop was golden
　　When I brought Mary home.

Now still down Reedy River
　　The grassy sheoaks sigh;
The waterholes still mirror
　　The pictures in the sky;
The golden sand is drifting
　　Across the rocky bars;
And over all for ever
　　Go sun and moon and stars.

But of the hut I builded
　　There are no traces now,
And many rains have levelled
　　The furrows of my plough.
The glad bright days have vanished;
　　For sombre branches wave
Their wattle-blossom golden
　　Above my Mary's grave.

REEDY RIVER
Oil on hardboard 14 in. × 18 in. 1973

The Water-Lily

A lonely young wife
In her dreaming discerns
A lily-decked pool
With a border of ferns,
And a beautiful child,
With butterfly wings,
Trips down to the edge of the water and sings:
"Come, mamma! come!
Quick! follow me!
Step out on the leaves of the water-lily!"

And the lonely young wife,
Her heart beating wild,
Cries, "Wait till I come,
Till I reach you, my child!"
But the beautiful child
With butterfly wings
Steps out on the leaves of the lily and sings:
"Come, mamma! come!
Quick! follow me!
And step on the leaves of the water-lily!"

And the wife in her dreaming
Steps out on the stream,
But the lily leaves sink
And she wakes from her dream.
Ah, the waking is sad,
For the tears that it brings,
And she knows 'tis her dead baby's spirit that sings:
"Come, mamma! come!
Quick! follow me!
Step out on the leaves of the water-lily!"

THE WATER-LILY
Oil on hardboard 14 in. × 18 in. 1973

The Blue Mountains

Above the ashes straight and tall,
  Through ferns with moisture dripping,
I climb beneath the sandstone wall,
  My feet on mosses slipping.

Like ramparts round the valley's edge
  The tinted cliffs are standing,
With many a broken wall and ledge,
  And many a rocky landing.

And round about their rugged feet
  Deep ferny dells are hidden
In shadowed depths, whence dust and heat
  Are banished and forbidden.

The stream that, crooning to itself,
  Comes down a tireless rover,
Flows calmly to the rocky shelf,
  And there leaps bravely over.

Now pouring down, now lost in spray
  When mountain breezes sally,
The water strikes the rock midway,
  And leaps into the valley.

Now in the west the colours change,
  The blue with crimson blending;
Behind the far Dividing Range
  The sun is fast descending.

And mellowed day comes o'er the place,
  And softens ragged edges;
The rising moon's great placid face
  Looks gravely o'er the ledges.

THE BLUE MOUNTAINS
Oil on hardboard 14 in. × 18 in. 1973

Taking His Chance

THEY stood by the door of the Inn on the Rise;
May Carney looked up in the bushranger's eyes:
"Oh! why did you come?—it was mad of you, Jack;
You know that the troopers are out on your track."
A laugh and a shake of his obstinate head—
"I wanted a dance, and I'll chance it," he said.

Some twenty-odd Bushmen had come to the ball,
But Jack from his youth had been known to them all,
And bushmen are soft where a woman is fair,
So the love of May Carney protected him there.
Through all the short evening—it seems like romance—
She danced with a bushranger taking his chance.

'Twas midnight—the dancers stood suddenly still,
For hoof-beats were heard on the side of the hill!
Ben Duggan, the drover, along the hillside
Came riding as only a bushman can ride.
He sprang from his horse, to the dancers he sped—
"The troopers are down in the gully!" he said.

Quite close to the shanty the troopers were seen.
"Clear out and ride hard for the ranges, Jack Dean!
Be quick!" said May Carney—her hand on her heart—
"We'll bluff them awhile, and 'twill give you a start."
He lingered a moment—to kiss her, of course—
Then ran to the trees where he'd hobbled his horse.

She ran to the gate, and the troopers were there—
The jingle of hobbles came faint on the air—
Then loudly she screamed: it was only to drown
The treacherous clatter of sliprails let down.
But troopers are sharp, and she saw at a glance
That someone was taking a desperate chance.

They chased, and they shouted, "Surrender, Jack Dean!"
They called him three times in the name of the Queen.
Then came from the darkness the clicking of locks;
The crack of a rifle was heard in the rocks!
A shriek, and a shout, and a rush of pale men—
And there lay the bushranger, chancing it then.

The sergeant dismounted and knelt on the sod—
"Your bushranging's over—make peace, Jack, with God!"
The dying man laughed—not a word he replied,
But turned to the girl who knelt down by his side.
He gazed in her eyes as she lifted his head:
"Just kiss me—my girl—and—I'll—chance it," he said.

TAKING HIS CHANCE
Oil on hardboard 14 in. × 18 in. 1973

To an Old Mate

OLD MATE! In the gusty old weather,
When our hopes and our troubles were new,
In the years spent in wearing out leather,
I found you unselfish and true—
I have gathered these verses together
For the sake of our friendship and you.

You may think for awhile, and with reason,
Though still with a kindly regret,
That I've left it full late in the season
To prove I remember you yet;
But you'll never judge me by their treason
Who profit by friends—and forget.

I remember, Old Man, I remember—
The tracks that we followed are clear—
The jovial last nights of December,
The solemn first days of the year,
Long tramps through the clearings and timber,
Short partings on platform and pier.

I can still feel the spirit that bore us,
And often the old stars will shine—
I remember the last spree in chorus
For the sake of that other Lang Syne
When the tracks lay divided before us,
Your path through the future and mine.

Through the frost-wind that cut like whip-lashes,
Through the ever-blind haze of the drought—
And in fancy at times by the flashes
Of light in the darkness of doubt—
I have followed the tent-poles and ashes
Of camps that we moved farther out.

You will find in these pages a trace of
That side of our past which was bright,
And recognize sometimes the face of
A friend who has dropped out of sight—
I send them along in the place of
The letters I promised to write.

TO AN OLD MATE
Oil on hardboard 14 in. × 18 in. 1973

On the Night Train

HAVE you seen the Bush by moonlight from the train go running by,
Here a patch of glassy water, there a glimpse of mystic sky?
Have you heard the still voice calling, yet so warm, and yet so cold:
"I'm the Mother-Bush that bore you! Come to me when you are old?'

Did you see the Bush below you sweeping darkly to the range,
All unchanged and all unchanging, yet so very old and strange!
Did you hear the Bush a-calling, when your heart was young and bold
"I'm the Mother-Bush that nursed you! Come to me when you are old?

Through the long, vociferous cutting as the night train swiftly sped,
Did you hear the grey Bush calling from the pine-ridge overhead:
"You have seen the seas and cities; all seems done, and all seems told;
I'm the Mother-Bush that loves you! Come to me, now you are old?"

ON THE NIGHT TRAIN
Oil on hardboard 14 in. × 18 in. 1973

Days When We Went Swimming

THE breezes waved the silver grass
  Waist-high along the siding,
And to the creek we ne'er could pass,
  Three boys, on bare back riding;
Beneath the sheoaks in the bend
  The waterhole was brimming—
Do you remember yet, old friend,
  The times we went in swimming?

The days we played the wag from school—
  Joys shared—but paid for singly—
The air was hot, the water cool—
  And naked boys are kingly!
With mud for soap, the sun to dry—
  A well-planned lie to stay us,
And dust well rubbed on neck and face
  Lest cleanliness betray us.

And you'll remember farmer Kutz—
  Though scarcely for his bounty—
He'd leased a forty-acre block,
  And thought he owned the county;
A farmer of the old-world school,
  That men grew hard and grim in,
He drew his water from the pool
  That we preferred to swim in.

And do you mind when down the creek
  His angry way he wended,
A green-hide cartwhip in his hand
  For our young backs intended?
Three naked boys upon the sand—
  Half-buried and half-sunning—
Three startled boys without their clothes
  Across the paddocks running.

We'd had some scares, but we looked blank
  When, resting there and chumming,
We glanced by chance along the bank
  And saw the farmer coming!
Some home impressions linger yet
  Of cups of sorrow brimming;
I hardly think that we'll forget
  The last day we went swimming.

DAYS WHEN WE WENT SWIMMING
Oil on hardboard 14 in. × 18 in. 1973

The Roaring Days

The night too quickly passes
  And we are growing old,
So let us fill our glasses
  And toast the Days of Gold;
When finds of wondrous treasure
  Set all the South ablaze,
And you and I were faithful mates
  All through the Roaring Days!

Then stately ships came sailing
  From every harbour's mouth,
And sought the Land of Promise
  That beaconed in the South;
Then southward streamed their streamers
  And swelled their canvas full
To speed the wildest dreamers
  E'er borne in vessel's hull.

Their shining El Dorado
  Beneath the southern skies
Was day and night for ever
  Before their eager eyes.
The brooding bush, awakened,
  Was stirred in wild unrest,
And all the year a human stream
  Went pouring to the West.

The rough bush roads re-echoed
  The bar-room's noisy din,
When troops of stalwart horsemen
  Dismounted at the inn.
And oft the hearty greetings
  And hearty clasp of hands
Would tell of sudden meetings
  of friends from other lands.

And when the cheery camp-fire
  Explored the bush with gleams,
The camping-grounds were crowded
  With caravans of teams;
Then home the jests were driven,
  And good old songs were sung,
And choruses were given
  The strength of heart and lung.

Oft when the camps were dreaming,
  And fires began to pale,
Through rugged ranges gleaming

THE ROARING DAYS
Oil on hardboard 14 in. × 18 in. 1973

Swept on the Royal Mail.
Behind six foaming horses,
    And lit by flashing lamps,
Old Cobb and Co., in royal state,
    Went dashing past the camps.

Oh, who would paint a goldfield,
    And paint the picture right,
As old Adventure saw it
    In early morning's light?
The yellow mounds of mullock
    With spots of red and white,
The scattered quartz that glistened
    Like diamonds in light;

The azure line of ridges,
    The bush of darkest green,
The little homes of calico
    That dotted all the scene.
The flat straw hats, with ribands.
    That old engravings show—
The dress that still reminds us
    Of sailors, long ago.

I hear the fall of timber
    From distant flats and fells,
The pealing of the anvils
    As clear as little bells,
The rattle of the cradle,
    The clack of windlass-boles,
The flutter of the crimson flags
    Above the golden holes.

Ah, then their hearts were bolder,
    And if Dame Fortune frowned
Their swags they'd lightly shoulder
    And tramp to other ground.
Oh, they were lion-hearted
    Who gave our country birth!
Stout sons, of stoutest fathers born,
    From all the lands on earth!

Those golden days are vanished,
  And altered is the scene;
The diggings are deserted,
  The camping-grounds are green;
The flaunting flag of progress
  Is in the West unfurled,
The mighty Bush with iron rails
  Is tethered to the world.